LAUBACH WAY TO
ENGLISH

NS 2
OK

LAUBACH WAY TO READING

Illustrations in this book are to be used by the teacher to show the student the meaning of vocabulary and structures introduced in conversations skills sections of the *ESL Teacher's Manual for Skill Book 2.*

For the teacher's convenience, words and sentences are given in small print to identify the pictures. These words and sentences can easily be covered if the teacher does not want the student to see them during conversation skills practice.

ISBN 978-0-88336-394-2

Copyright © 1991, 1981, 1977 New Readers Press
New Readers Press
A Publishing Division of ProLiteracy
1320 Jamesville Avenue, Syracuse, New York 13210
www.newreaderspress.com

Printed in the United States of America
20   19   18   17   16   15   14   13   12   11
10   9   8

Illustrated by Glenda Rogers

All proceeds from the sale of New Readers Press materials support literacy programs in the United States and worldwide.

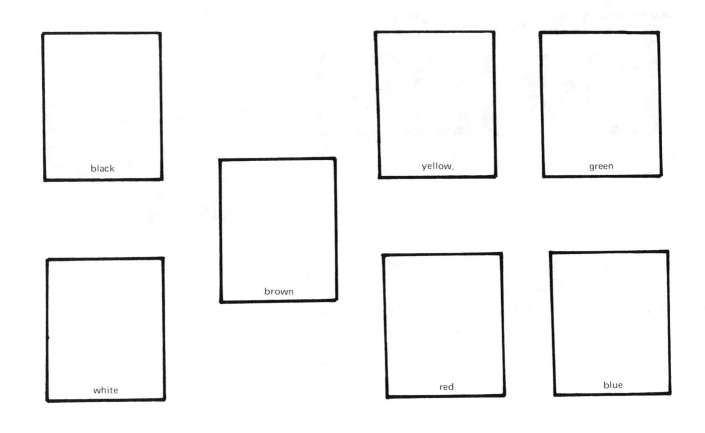

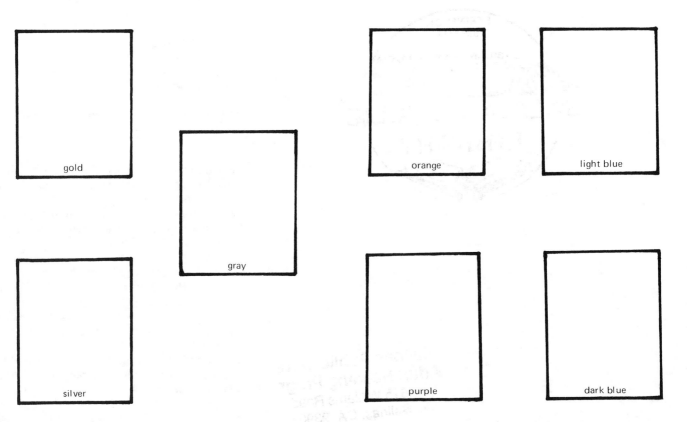

Colors

Jill Hill

Kim Hill

coat

jacket

belt

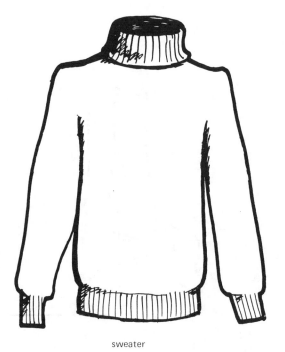

sweater

ring

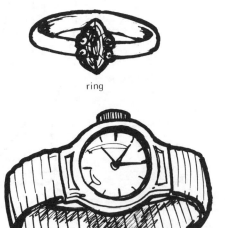

watch

Clothes

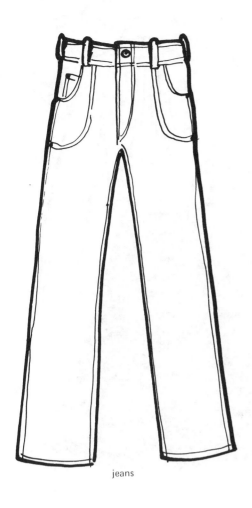

jeans

pants

glasses

shoes

5

dress

blouse

skirt

suit

shirt

tie

6

a whistle

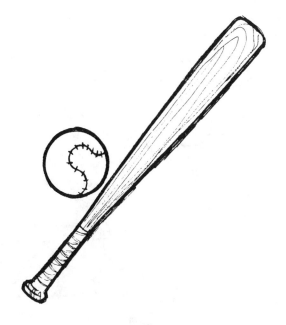

a bat and a ball

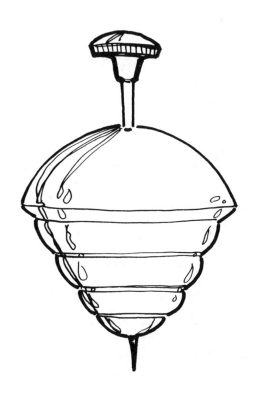

a top

Toys

a doll

The Hills live in this house.

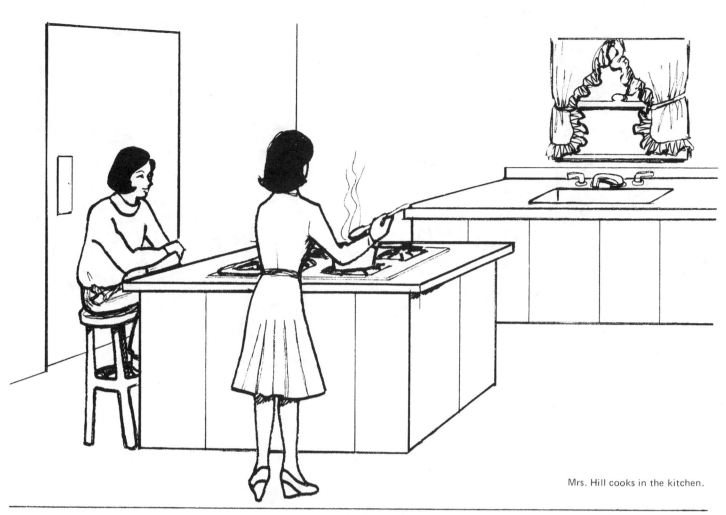

Mrs. Hill cooks in the kitchen.

The Hills eat and drink in the dining room.

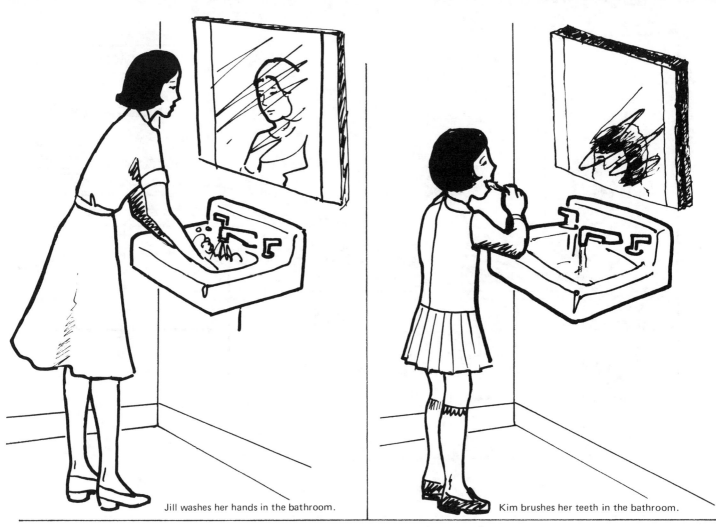

Jill washes her hands in the bathroom.

Kim brushes her teeth in the bathroom.

They sit and talk in the living room.
They watch television in the living room.

Mr. and Mrs. Hill are sleeping in the bedroom.

Ed puts his clothes in the closet.

My sister has a picture of her baby.

My friend has a lily on the table.

My girl friend is pretty.

My boy friend is handsome.

My neighbor has roses.

My boss has flowers on his desk.

This is a city.

Kitty lives in a big building in the city.

Kitty goes to the library for books.

Kitty goes to English classes at the school.

Kitty goes to the hospital in the afternoon.
She's a nurse.

Kitty and Jimmy put money in the bank.

They send letters and buy stamps at the post office.

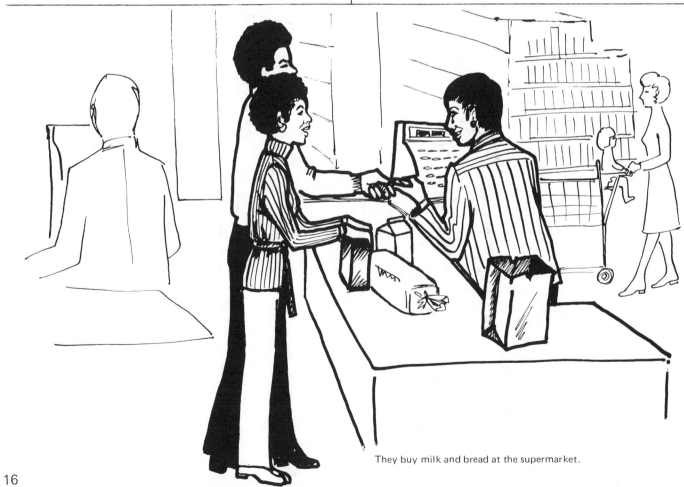

They buy milk and bread at the supermarket.

They buy clothes at the department store.

They go to church on Sunday.

17

The man is big.
The child is little.

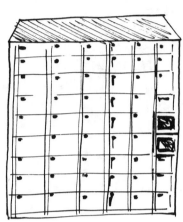

The building is small.

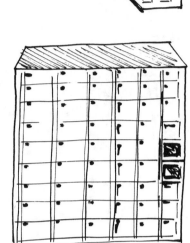

The building is big.

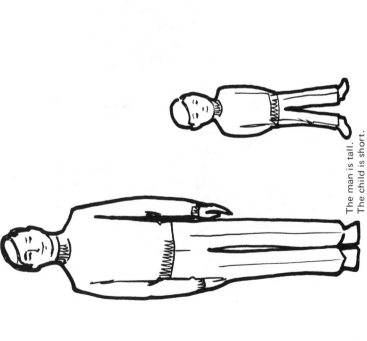

The man is tall.
The child is short.

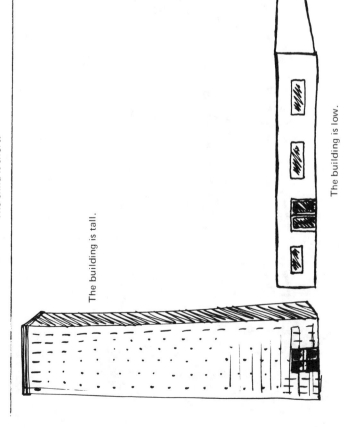

The building is tall.

The building is low.

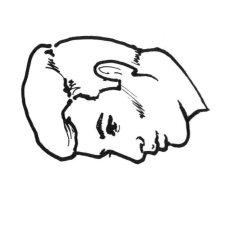

The man is handsome.

The building is ugly.

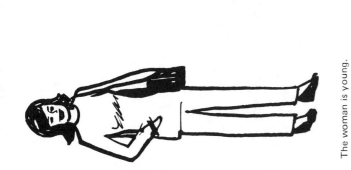

The woman is pretty.

The man is old.

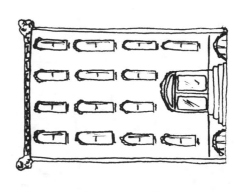

The building is old.

The woman is young.

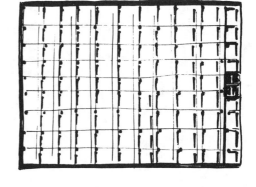

The building is new.

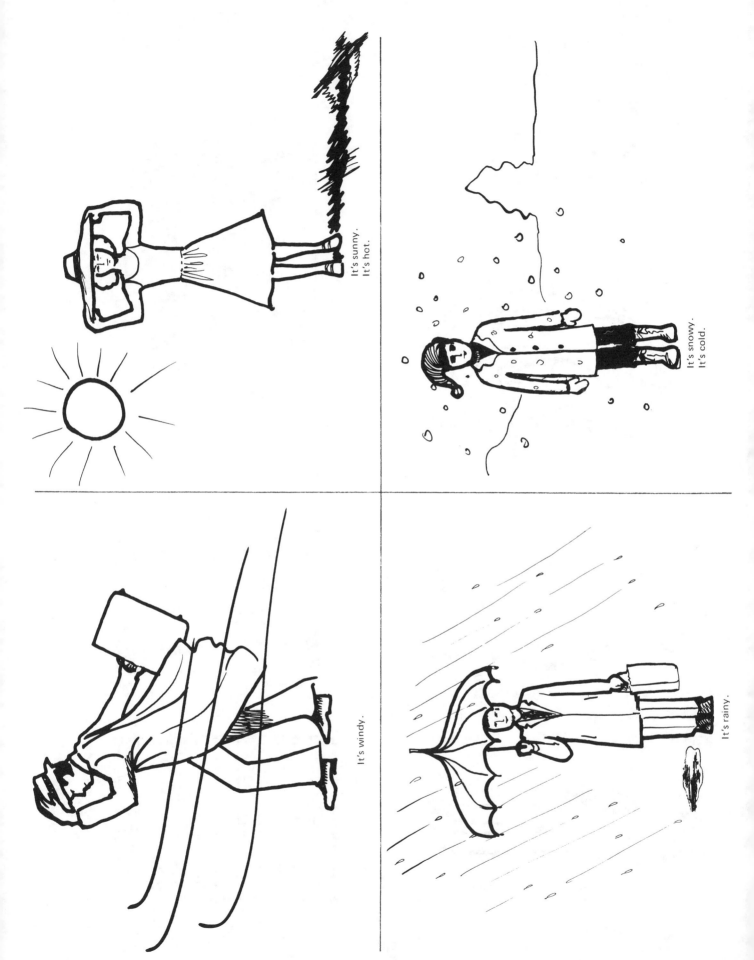

It's sunny.
It's hot.

It's snowy.
It's cold.

It's windy.

It's rainy.

The duck is in the mud.

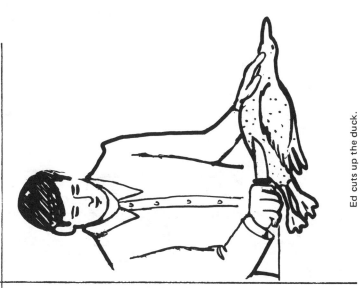

Ed cuts up the duck.

Ed hits a duck.

He brings the duck to the tent.

The sun is up.
Glenn Hill is hunting with his son.
They are hunting ducks with guns.

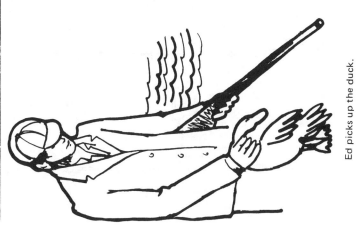

Ed picks up the duck.

21

This is a kitchen.
There is a pan on the stove.

There are cups in the sink.
There is a rug on the floor.

There is a light on the ceiling.
There is a telephone on the wall.

There are dishes in the cabinet.

There is bread on the counter.

There is milk in the refrigerator.

The man is getting thin.

The woman is getting fat.

The man is getting old.

The taxi is getting stuck in the mud.

The man is getting in the car.

The man is getting out of the taxi.

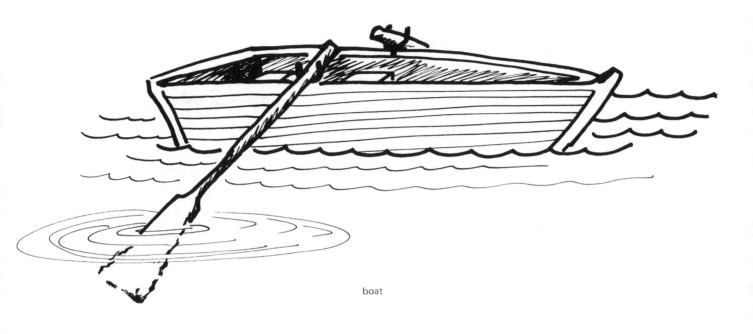

boat

truck

The man is getting on the bus.

The man is getting off the airplane.

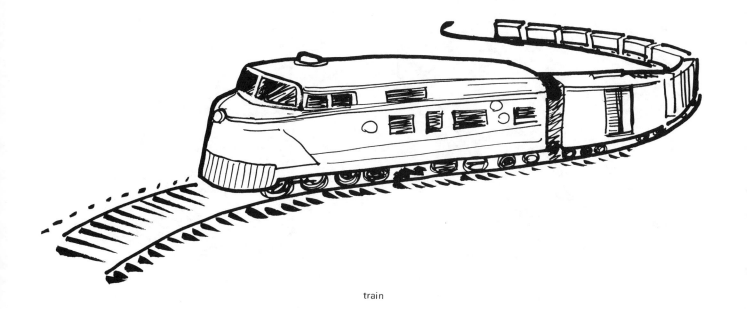

train

bicycle

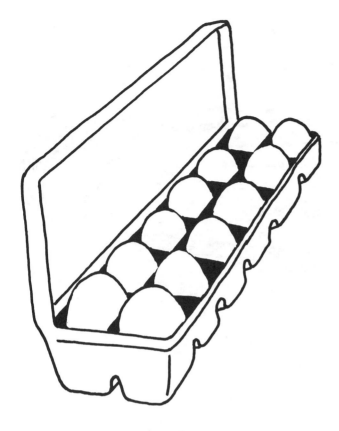

carton of eggs

can of coffee

box of cereal

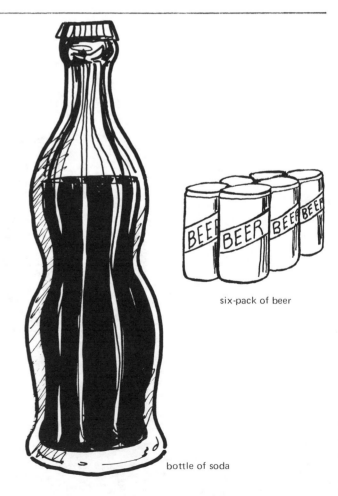

six-pack of beer

bottle of soda

carton of ice cream

package of cookies

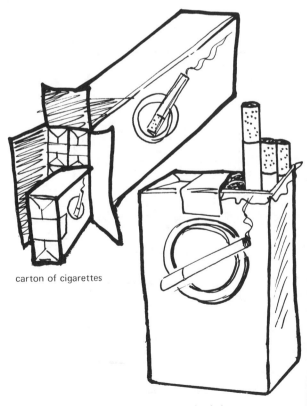

carton of cigarettes

pack of cigarettes

jar of jelly

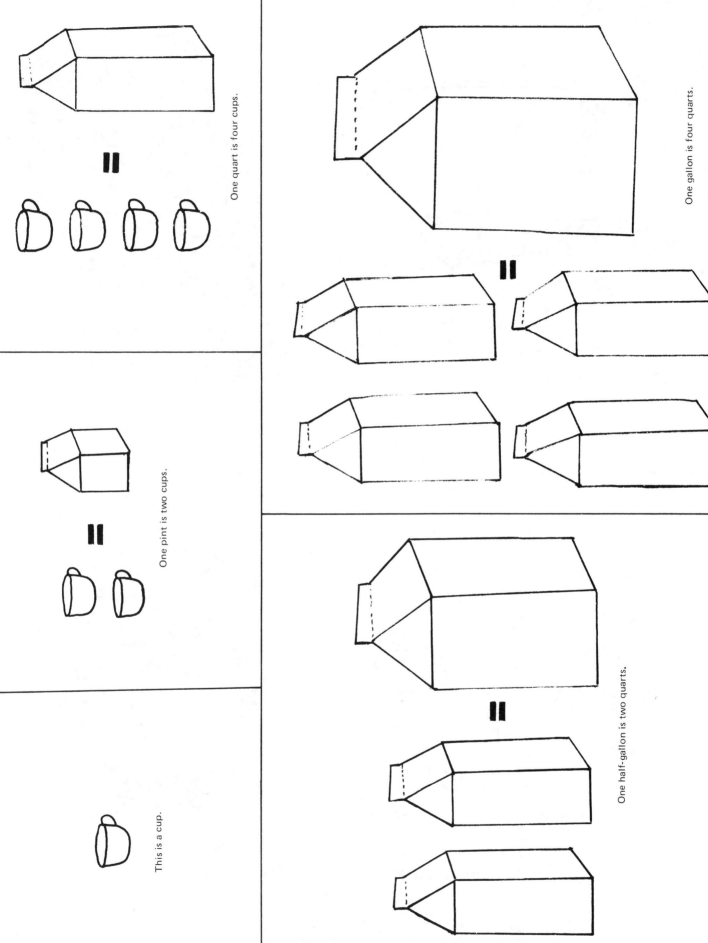

One quart is four cups.

One pint is two cups.

This is a cup.

One gallon is four quarts.

One half-gallon is two quarts.

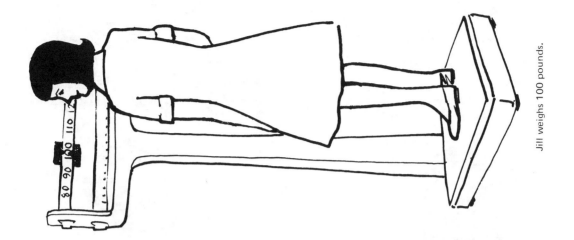

Jill weighs 100 pounds.

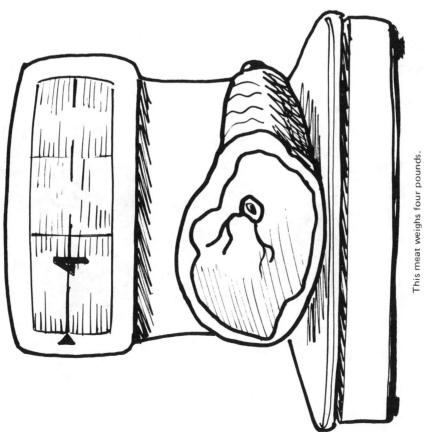

This meat weighs four pounds.

The church bell is ringing.

The dinner bell is ringing.

The doorbell is ringing.

The telephone is ringing.

These are hens. The hens are sitting on their nests.

We get eggs from hens.

The girl is in bed.
She's sick.

The girl is getting up.
She's well.

The boy walks to the store.
He's slow.

The boy runs to the store.
He's fast.

a lot of eggs
many eggs

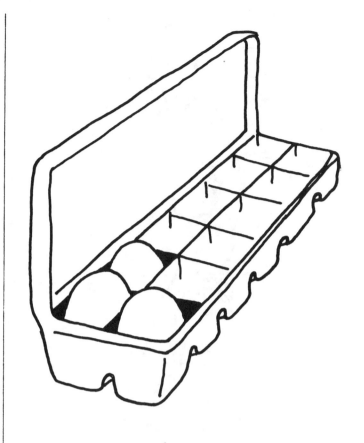

a few eggs

a lot of apples
many apples

a few apples

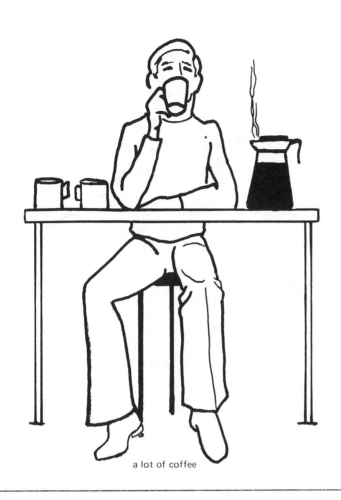

a lot of coffee

a little coffee

a lot of money

a little money

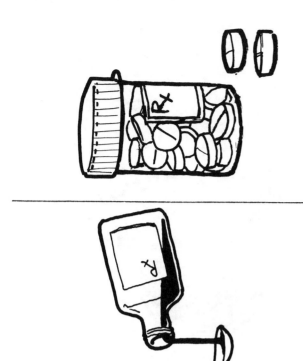

He takes aspirin for his headache.
He takes pills for his earache.

Mr. Hunt takes a teaspoon of medicine for his sore throat.

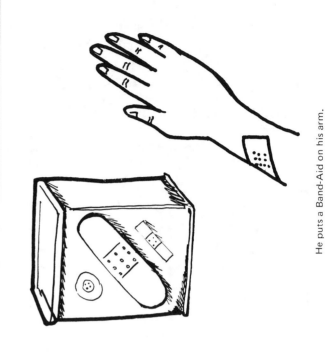

He puts a Band-Aid on his arm.

Mr. Hunt takes his temperature with a thermometer.

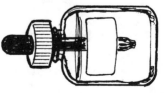

He puts nosedrops in his nose.

The black cat kills the rat.

The cat lives. The cat is alive.

The rat dies. The rat is dead.

This is a rat.

a shopping bag

a bag
a suitcase

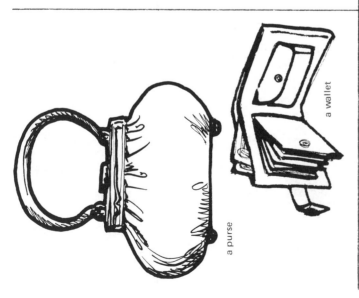

a basket

a briefcase

a purse

a wallet

a lunch box

40

The children are sitting on the stairs.

The woman's sitting on the bench.

The friends are sitting on the sofa.

He's sitting on the rock.

She's sitting on the grass.

The man's sitting on the chair.

The boys are sitting on the floor.

Ford Motor Co.

This is a car factory. The workers make cars.

Tonka Toys

This is a toy factory. The workers make toys.

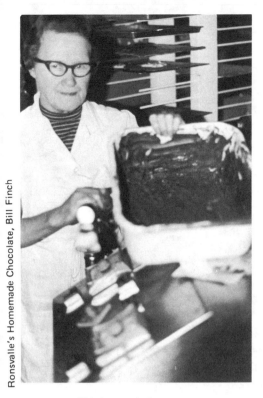

This is a candy factory.
The workers make candy.

This is a paper factory.
The workers make paper.

This a glass factory.
The workers make glass.

The teacher works in a classroom.

Dr. Chan works in an office.

The patient sits in the doctor's waiting room.

He's washing his hands in the men's room.

She's combing her hair in the ladies' room.

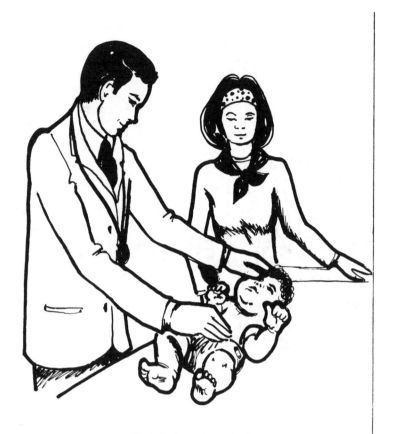

The baby is getting a checkup.

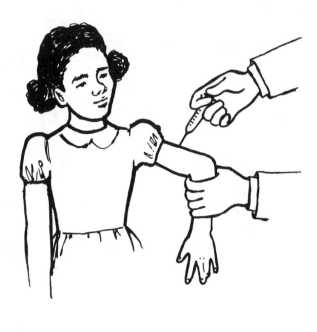

Molly is getting a shot in her arm.

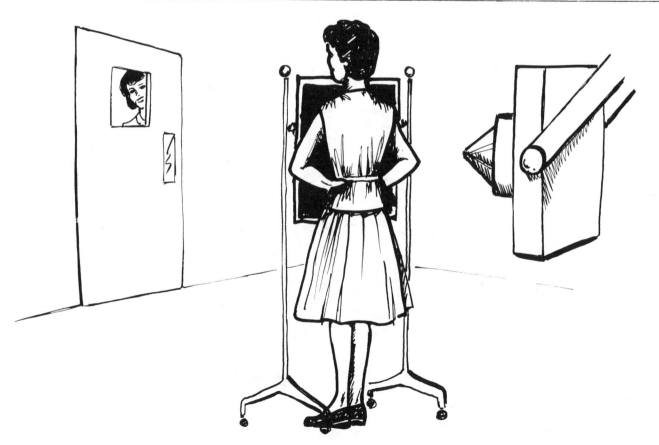

Mrs. Roberts is getting a chest x-ray.

Tom and Don do the dishes.

Mrs. Roberts does the laundry.

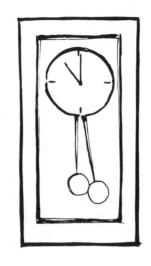

The clock stopped.

Tom will fix the clock.

The lock won't open.

Tom will fix the lock.

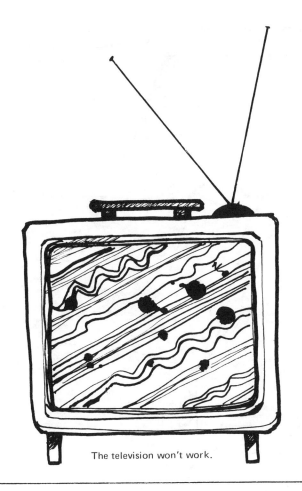

The television won't work.

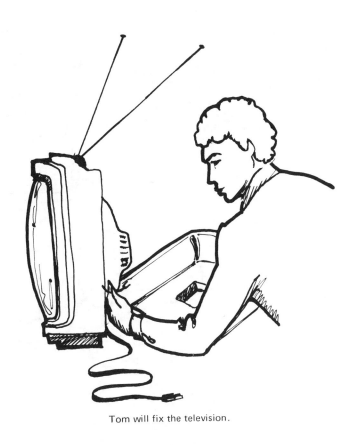

Tom will fix the television.

The top is broken.

Tom will fix the top.

Living Room Furniture

stitches
stitched up

Injuries

Carl Arthur works on a farm.
Mr. Arthur is a farmer.

There's a big red barn on his farm.

Carmen Arthur has a garden.
Mrs. Arthur is a gardener.

Her garden is between the house and the garage.

The Arthurs go to the farmers' market every week.

Mr. Arthur sells eggs and apples.   Mrs. Arthur sells bread and jars of jelly.

Mr. Smith went into the house.

He went up the stairs.   Mrs. Smith went down the stairs.

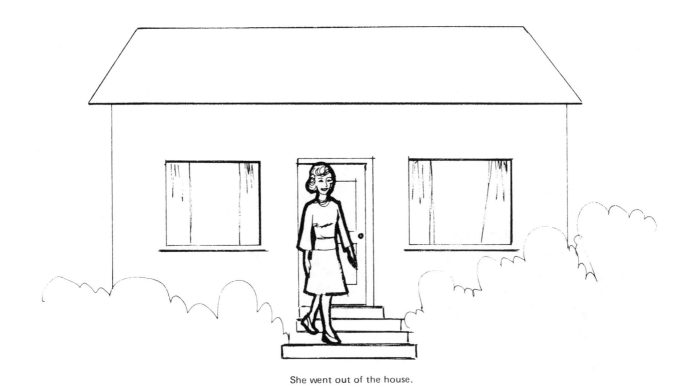

She went out of the house.

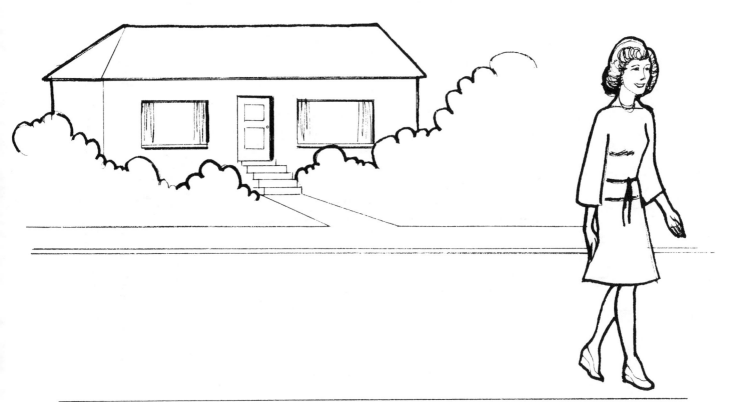

She walked across the street.

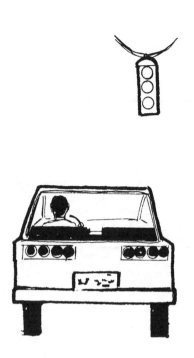

He stops at the red light.

He parks his car in the parking lot.

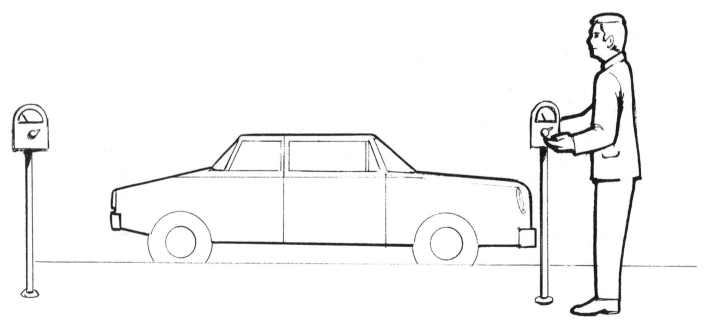

Bob parks his car on the street.
He puts a quarter in the parking meter.

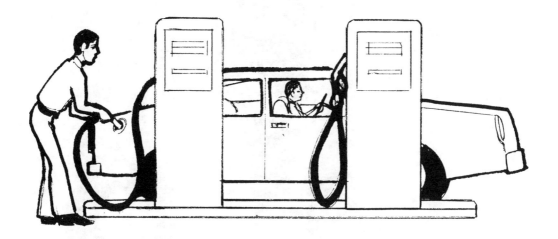

He stops at a gas station to buy gas for his car.

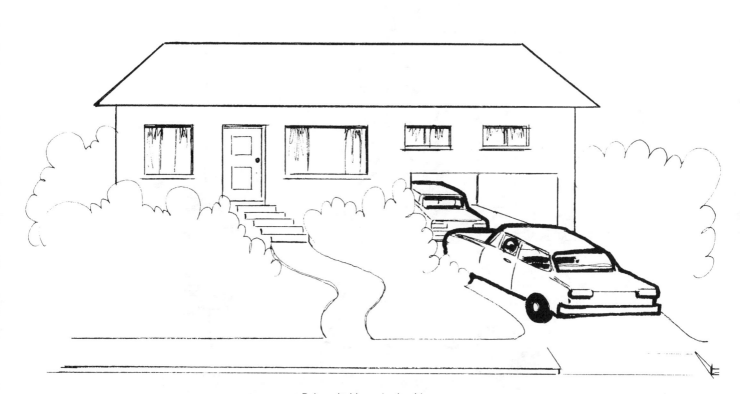

Bob parks his car in the driveway.
His wife's car is in the garage.

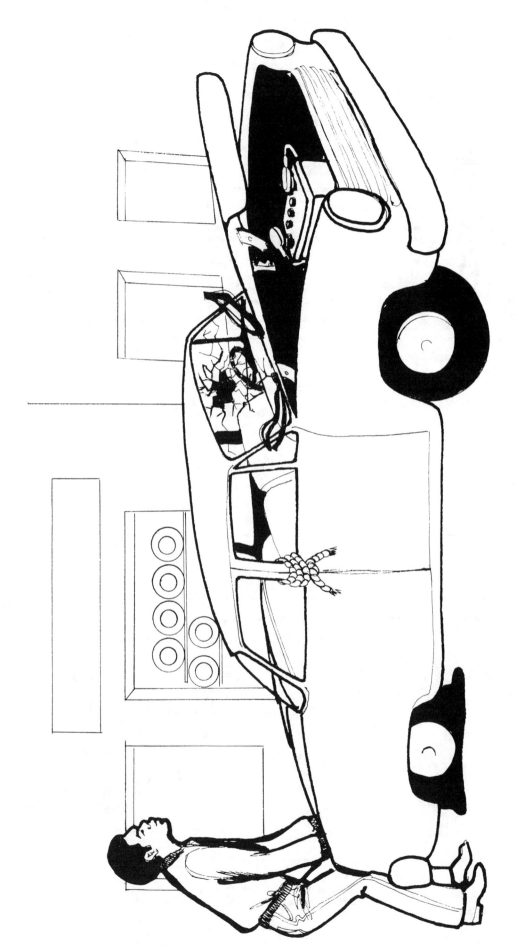

Jimmy's car is at the repair shop.

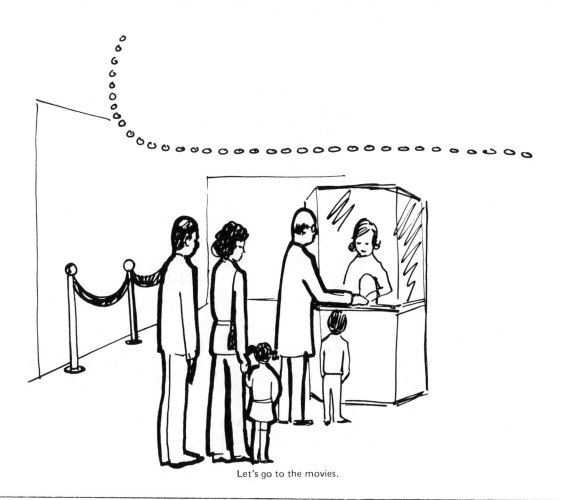

Let's go to the movies.

Let's go to the party.

Let's go to a restaurant.

Let's go to a concert.

Let's go on a picinic.

Let's go for a walk.

Traffic is heavy.
There's a traffic cop.

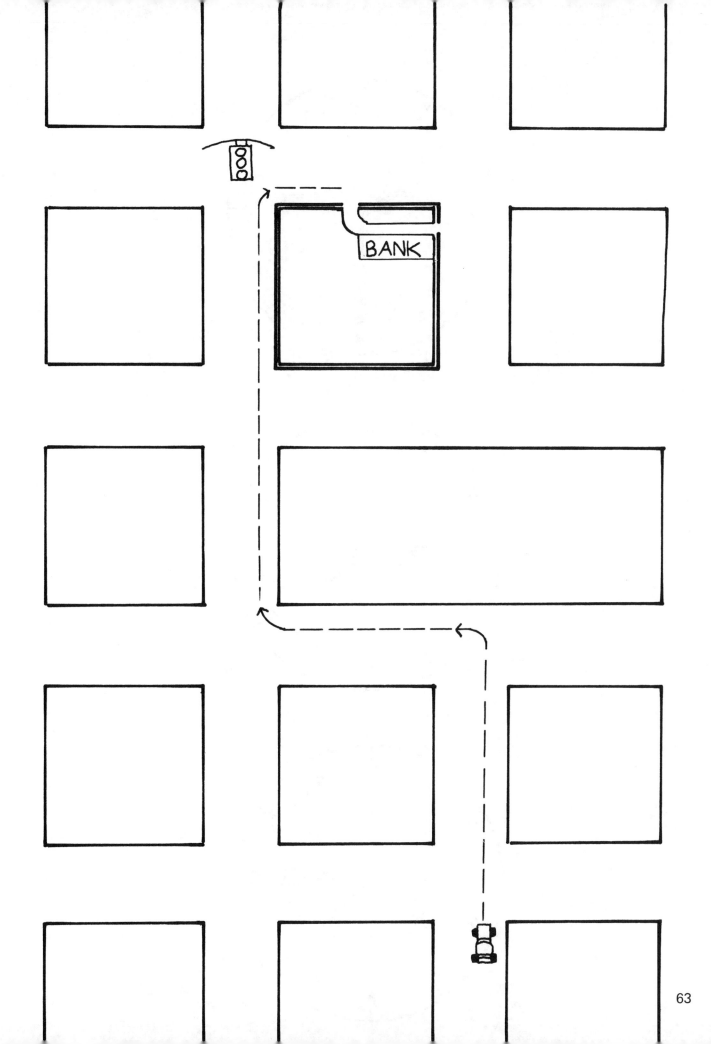

BANK

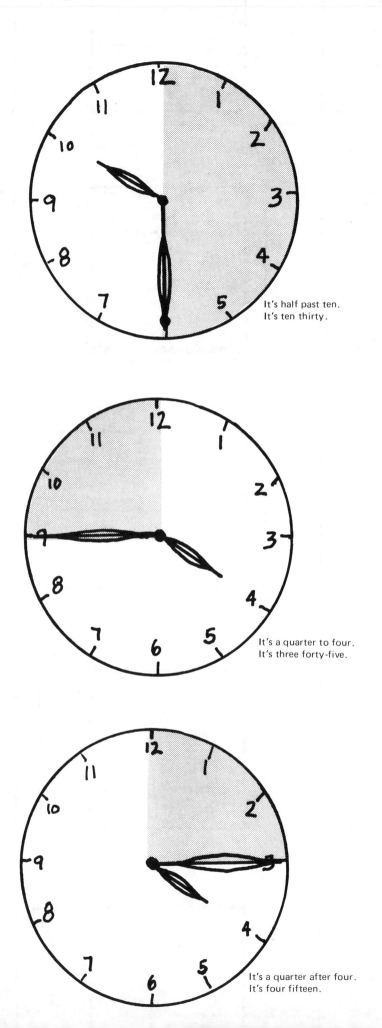

It's half past ten.
It's ten thirty.

It's a quarter to four.
It's three forty-five.

It's a quarter after four.
It's four fifteen.